Horsemanship

What does horsemanship mean to you?
Quotes from Riders Around the World
Volume I

Gina McKnight

Illustrated by Zorka Veličković

Monday Creek Publishing
Ohio USA

For the love of horses.

Journey with me through country stables, city trails, working round pens, and shining arenas where you will find equestrian wisdom from around the world. *"What does horsemanship mean to you?"* The question asked of cowboys, horse trainers, clinicians, equine writers, eventers, bull riders, barrel racers, and more! As a freelance writer, I have the great opportunity to connect with amazing horsemen and horsewomen. They are the inspiration for this book. To read their entire interview, visit www.ginamc.blogspot.com. My thanks to each one for their contribution to this volume.

Special thanks to Zorka for inspiration and motivation. Her charismatic character, along with her engaging art, continue to encourage and support our love for horses.

We are thrilled to donate a portion of the proceeds from this book to local horse rescues.

Gina McKnight

Contents

Horsemanship to me means taking care of your own horse and knowing your horse. It means cleaning his stall (maybe not every day but often), grooming him, bathing him, feeding him, scheduling and holding him for the vet and farrier, cleaning his tack, braiding him, washing his saddle pads at home in your dryer, sending in entries, preparing him for the ring, driving the trailer to the shows. I always took care of my own horse when I was competing and it was the best. That's how I learned the most about horsemanship. When I was 17 or 18, I'd load up the trailer and go off to an away show by myself for a week. I'd try to stable near my trainer, but I wasn't technically "with" their barn. It was hard work and a lot of responsibility, but there is nothing better than being solely in charge of your own horse's care. I know not everyone can do their own work, but I think everyone should have had to do it in their riding career at some point. And not just for one show, but for a year or something. There is so much more to competing than what you do in the saddle.

Kim Ablon-Whitney
Massachusetts, USA
Equestrian, United States Equestrian Federation (USEF) 'R' Judge
Author of *Blue Ribbons*
www.kimablonwhitney.com

I suppose I would define horsemanship as one's rapport with the horse; one's ability to work around them, and with them to get a job done. It is a process of noticing their nature and honing one's skills until ultimately there is a sense of teamwork; of purpose for both parties. Like visual art or music, it is a lifetime of learning, and striving to do better.

Jean Abernethy
Ontario, Canada
Creator and Author of *Fergus the Horse*
www.jeanabernethy.com
www.fergusthehorse.com

To me horsemanship means two-way communication between horse and rider based on mutual trust, respect, and affection. It is more than physical communication, it is mental and emotional as well. Horsemanship leads to an intuitive connection so that communication requires no conscious thought.

Lee Atterbury
Wisconsin, USA
Equestrian
Author of *Big Fracking Mess*
www.leeatterbury.com

Horsemanship is nothing more than relationship. Some folks are rotten friends or co-workers and a bunch of people who have horses are no better. I consider "Horsemanship" the term for excellence in relationship with horses. It is considerate, intentional, founded in knowledge, and is the perfect balance of authority, humility, and accountability. Horsemanship offers, it does not demand.

Lynn Baber
Equestrian, Equine Clinician
National and International Horse Breeder
Author of *Amazing Grays, Amazing Grace*
www.lynnbaber.com

Horsemanship is satisfying the needs of each horse. From the basics to advanced management under the rigors of competition. Horsemanship also means looking beyond the game...and taking care of our responsibility to each equine athlete, both during and after their careers.

Seth Benzel
New York, USA
Abstract Deconstructionist
Proprietor of *AmDubai Racing Stable*
www.sbenzel75.faso.com

Horsemanship is the desire to understand horses mentally, physically and spiritually in order to create willing and harmonic partnerships with joint goals.

Catherine Louise Birmingham

Italy
International Acclaimed Dressage Rider, Trainer, Healer and Writer
Author of *Ride for Life: The Three Golden Principles for Riders*
www.catherinelouisebirmingham.com

To me, horsemanship starts with good healthcare of the horse. Then it is in building of trust and also to gain the respect from the horse on the ground. When you start with getting a horse's trust and having them respect you on the ground, it makes them so much more responsive when you get in the saddle and start working with them. Unfortunately, horses with no ground manners or respect for their rider is something I see a lot of when I am at shows. It's also usually the main problem I deal with when someone sends me a horse that they are having problems with. I strive to educate more people on the importance of ground work, its where trust and bond between horse and rider will start to build. It's something that requires a lot of dedication and patience for because it is not something that happens quickly; it takes time, a lot of energy, and it can really get frustrating at times. But I can tell you this, the work is all worth it. To me it is the best feeling in the world and if I had to do it all over again, I would.

LeAnna BigTown Billie
Florida, USA
All Around Rodeo Champion
www.facebook.com/bigtown.billie1

Horsemanship is the communication, confidence, balance and harmony between horse and rider.

Monica Bonaccorso
Sicily, Italy
Equestrian, Sicily Horse Riding
www.sicilyhorseriding.com

Horsemanship to me is being experienced, and knowledgeable in the equine industry. It is also knowing how to care for the horses you have and being able to doctor on them when needed.

Barry Brown
South Carolina, USA
Professional Rodeo Cowboys Association Comeback Cowboy
Author of *The Bionic Bullrider*
www.bionicbullrider.com

Horsemanship means being the best rider you can be -
both mentally and physically. If we're not eating well and
giving our body what it needs, we are not at our best. We
expect our horses to perform at their best and feed them
accordingly, now it's time to do the same for ourselves.
Horsemanship is also a way of life. It's being dedicated,
excited and being part of a community that stands together and stands for excellence. This is why we are so
proud and excited to introduce IsaEquine into this
world.

Tab Calvitti and Jenna Knudsen
New York, USA
Equestrians and the Proprietors of IsaEquine
www.isaequine.com

What does horsemanship mean to you?

For me, horsemanship is the ultimate expression of the bond that can be nurtured between horse and human. It represents a mutually beneficial journey between horse and human, each the better for the journey/relationship. Each half of the partnership must set aside their primal instincts for the relationship to be successful. Together they can accomplish so much more than individually. Watching that beautiful dance of a bareback and bridle-less ride is always moving to me.

Lisa Carter
Texas, USA
Equestrian, Equine Massage Therapist
Author of *A Prescription for Parelli*
www.heavenlygaitsequinemassage.com

Just what the word means = horse/man relationship. It is a dialogue between horses and men. Answers from our horses will depend greatly on our signs, and on the surroundings. Each horse/moment/scenario are different. We must be conscious on all unconscious acts.

Ignacio Alfredo Casafus
World Equestrian
Horse Trainer, Equine Ethology, Riding Instructor

For years and years, I had horses. Horsemanship is something that you either have or you don't have. It is very hard to learn. You can take lessons and everything, but if you don't have a relationship with the animal, you are not a horseman. You have to understand the animal and give it time to tell you what it needs, or don't. I was a trail rider for years and years. I went backpacking up in the mountains with friends. We used to take off and go for weekends in the high Sierras. It is a getaway time, really relaxing and it is fun to get out there with your horse, and the horse loves it, too. You have to cross rivers and all of that. I put all of that horsemanship, all of that information and knowledge I have about horses, in my books. Nothing pisses me off more to read a book where the rider of the horse is galloping, galloping, galloping, then pulls up in front of a store, jumps off the horse and leaves it standing there. That is not how it works. That is the impression that most movies and western books give you. They never took the time to take care of the animals. In all of my books, whether protagonist or antagonist, they all take time to take care of their animals before they do anything for themselves.

Jim Christina
California, USA
Host of LA Talk Radio's The Writer's Block
Author of *Contraband Cowboys*
www.jimchristina.net

Horsemanship means to me trust, respect, courage and companionship between man and horse. A complete understanding of one another's abilities, strengths and weaknesses.

Gordie Church
Nairobi, Kenya
Equestrian, Professional Safari Guide
www.safarisunlimited.com

I would say that horsemanship to me means loving the hobby and loving the horses, you don't have to be a cowboy or a pro rider, you just need to enjoy the horse and treat them well and the horse will enjoy you. People need to know that horses need to trust the people that ride them as much as the people need to trust the horse they ride.

Dr. Claudia Ciugudean, D.V.M.
Transylvania, Romania
Veterinarian, Equestrian
Vice President, Romanian Equine Veterinarian Association
www.romaniatrails.ro
www.ecvet.ro

I have to admit that I have never been a good rider, I'm better on the ground taking notes or photos. So, for me horsemanship means the quiet and subtle rapport that others have with horses, whether trainers, sport competitors, or leisure riders. Their ability to bond with a horse has been a central theme of my reporting and now in my fiction writing.

I have watched many proponents of horsemanship and they often had their own techniques. Yet they all share that quiet approach with subtle use of aids, so they seem to have a unified mind with the horse. Whenever I see such a rider enter an arena, there is a touch of magic.

If I had to choose one rider, it would be from the sport that I covered most, eventing. That horsemaster would be William Fox-Pitt, who is able to seem at one with almost any horse. He is also the most approachable and modest of people.

Roland Clarke
Idaho, USA
Author of *Spiral Hooves*
www.rolandclarke.com

Horsemanship means knowing and caring for every aspect of that horse. Putting your hands on the horse and knowing when something is different. Knowing your horse so well that you can visually tell when something is wrong even if no one else can. Knowing about anatomy and physiology, training, groundwork, riding, nutrition, fitness. Being a fair and equal partner to the horse and always keeping the health and welfare of the horse in mind. Being firm but fair. Understanding that you will never know all there is to know about horses and being open to learn more from other people and other horses. Never ever letting your ego or your emotions run your relationship with your horse.

Stephanie Corum
USA
Equestrian, Freelance Writer
Author of *Goats with Coats* and *Antics in the Attic*
Proprietor and Editor *Arabian Finish Line*
www.theridingwriter.com
www.arabianfinishline.com

What does horsemanship mean to you?

To me horsemanship is being in the same place as your horse, not physically but mentally being in the same place. It is about mutual respect between you and your horse. It is about understanding each other

Curt Courtney
USA
Equestrian
www.doubletaketrailersales.com

Whenever I think of horsemanship I think of that connection between horse and rider. The communication and understanding going back and forth between two very different individuals because the trust is so strong is such an amazing thing to experience. I think it's that feeling that always has people climbing back onto a horse even after they might have every reason to walk away. I don't own a horse, but I keep coming back and getting on, because that's just what I need to do.

Mara Dabrishus
USA
Equestrian, Author
Author of *Stay the Distance*
www.maradabrishus.com

There are a hundred definitions of horsemanship. The ability to bond with the horse and have the horse respond and respect you is the ultimate definition for me. Whatever the horse is doing - jumping, pulling a plow, or working cattle - the important part is the bond between the rider and the horse.

H. Alan Day
USA
Rancher, Author, Equestrian, Wild Mustang Advocate
Author of *The Horse Lover*
www.thehorselover.com

Horsemanship is a wonderful thing; man should be doing it with lots of love. It is very difficult to describe what it is for someone: horsemanship, it should be felt.

Ivan Dimitrijevic
Belgrade, Serbia
Equestrian, Horse Trainer

Horsemanship to me is, discovering myself, finding the inner Horseman/person I want to be, with the relationship of a horse. Being a part of something bigger than myself, doing something I'm only able to do because of the horse.

Justin Dunn
USA
Equestrian and Horse Trainer
www.justindunnhorsemanship.com

Paul Clark, Circa 1920s
Bradford, Pennsylvania USA
Photo Courtesy Peggy Jo Clark

Horsemanship is not doing the wrong thing, which we have all done! If you are in a bad mood don't go working your horse, you will not do the job properly, your horse will sense it and you will end up giving yourself three times more than you need to and making a mess of it. Come back after an hour when you are feeling less agitated. Once you have started something though you cannot walk away keep going to the end and have patience. Take the time to get to know your horse, watch him or her, learn and that means from the horse or from someone who gives you sound advice. The thing about horses is friendship and trust but also being the boss, quite a hard combination to find a happy medium. Be kind but firm, have understanding and discipline and always remember your horse can teach you as much if not more than you can teach them.

Chris Dyer
United Kingdom
Author of *Sting in the Tail*
www.chrisdyerauthor.com

The art of riding is a subtle communication between man and horse, where man must both exert control and let go of overt control. Horsemanship is finding the path of training that allows your horse to be the best it can be, no matter what discipline.

Zan Economopoulos
Georgia, USA
Equestrian and Fine Artist
www.whymzee.com

Traditionally, horsemanship has meant the art of riding but what I've discovered as my connection with horses has evolved over the decades, is that true horsemanship encompasses the entire relationship with them. Though there is much to be learned in the saddle, there are equally important lessons to be mastered from the ground, whether teaching another to ride, grooming, caring for them, or simply observing them. So, when I think of horsemanship, I consider it a whole-horse approach. This can truly deepen a horse and rider's relationship and create lasting bonds that will resonate for a lifetime.

Rachael Eliker
Nebraska, USA
Equestrian and Author
www.rachaeleliker.com

Horsemanship means not only understanding the needs of a horse, but being able to make decisions which are based on the needs of the horse, not of the rider/owner. Unfortunately, these days we see to many people willing to overlook what's best for the horse in favor of their own needs, something which I don't think any true horseman or horsewoman would ever do.

Adam Ellis
United Kingdom
Proprietor of Adam Ellis Saddles of UK Saddles Ltd
www.uksaddlesltd.com

In a nutshell, it means *everything*. Without it nothing can happen. Horsemanship is always a two-way street. Both horse owner and farrier must be devoted to it and practice it in order to do the best for our horses. A book published in 1889 titled: *The Practical Horseshoer* by M.T. Richardson is a good example of the importance of being a good horseman, first and a horseshoer, second. Many people forget that the art of horseshoeing is best performed when the farrier has the whole horse in mind. Horsemanship is like any other tool in a farrier's box, it must be honed or sharpened from time-to-time to give the best results.

Bryan Farcus
Ohio, USA
Farrier
www.farrierfriendly.com

I think horsemanship means the companionship between you and your horse. It's a bond like a friendship
and how well you can work and get along together. If you
pay attention to each other, then they will take care of
you just as much as you take care of them.

Melissa Fisher
Ohio, USA
Happy Hands Equine Massage LLC

Horsemanship means having a deeply personal relation-ship with your mount. Having horses and riding them is meaningless if you don't celebrate them as individuals. That's the best lesson horses teach *us* that life isn't all about *our* needs and *our* wants. We have to remember it's a two-way street - we practice horsemanship but our horses have to practice humanship!

Heidi Furseth
Washington, USA
Equestrian
Author of *Easy Love*
www.easylovehorses.com

I believe horses do as much for if not more for us then we can ever do for them. We must respect that it is always the rider's decision to pursue athletic endeavors and individual care needed to keep them happy in their work. We need to understand that horse's social behaviors are based on a hierarchy and we need to insert ourselves in that system as a leader. Riders who do not set themselves as a leader risk damaging the horse's confidence and losing the horse's respect for you. I have not been drawn towards natural horsemanship or the Parelli method. I keep my requests simple and consistent so that I can interact with my horse with kindness, but as a leader.

Marley Filiptseva
Ontario, Canada
Proprietor of Keystone Dressage
www.keystonedressage.com

Horsemanship is the art of understanding horse psychology and connecting with them through a language they can understand, and by doing so, strive to provide them with their daily needs and comforts while riding as well as for the rest of their days.

Anish Gajjar
India
Equestrian Trainer and Consultant, Owner of Silver Studs
www.anishgajjar.com

Clancy in *The Man from Snowy River* is a good example of a horseman: someone who partners with his or her horse. A horseman knows that you never stop learning and that a well-treated horse is a joy to work with and ride. A horseman treats horses with respect and listens to the horse but also knows that he is the head of this herd of two. A horseman makes sure the horse's needs are met for everything from health to safety, and a horseman treats others with respect and isn't afraid to both learn and to share knowledge and experience. A horseman is a good example for other horsemen. A really excellent horseman speaks horse—I aspire to this ideal.

Sally Gerard
Author, Equestrian, Poet, English Teacher
Author of *Windows in the Loft*
www.sygoerner.wordpress.com

Horsemanship means for me the relationship between teacher and student. In this relationship I am the student and the horse is my teacher! Horses are my relaxing... Horses give me wings to fly.

Ali Ghoorchian
Tehran, Iran
Equestrian, Horseback Archer
Director, Shabdiz Horseback Archery and Trail Center
www.ShabdizEquestrianCenter.com

Forming a bond with the horse on the ground before you ride, having empathy for the horse and working with and riding the horse as naturally as possible. Communication in a manner that the horse understands and responds to willingly is, I believe, the key.

Cheryl Giacchetti
Port Elizabeth Area, South Africa
Equestrian, Horseback Riding Tour Guide
Founding Board Member, Mkulu Kei Horse Trails & Riding Holidays cc
www.mkulukeihorsetrails.co.za

Horsemanship to me is establishing a bond between you and a horse. Being able to communicate and work *with* a horse is something few people can do, but once you establish that level of trust and camaraderie with a horse, there's no feeling quite like it. It's not about taking command of the horse, it's about making them want to follow you and trust you. I don't consider myself an expert horseman, but I've found the horses I can establish a foundation of trust and friendship with, tend to be the horses I work best with.

Nolan Gillies
Idaho, USA
Professional Rodeo Cowboy

Jack Clark, Circa 1930s
At the Livery Barn
Bradford, Pennsylvania USA
Photo Courtesy Peggy Jo Clark

It means natural horsemanship. Working with the horse with respect and consideration in his physical, mental, emotional and spiritual aspects without using force.

Mandy Hall
United Kingdom
Proprietor of Equine Well Being Management
www.equinewellbeingmanagement.com

To me, horsemanship is learning all you can, and to give the best you can. To listen to all the advice that is given, and pick and choose what works for you. To respect the opinions of others and their experiences.

Never think you are better than anyone, because there is always someone better than you. Never set your horse up to fail. Take the time to help others if asked because you were there yourself once. To provide the best care for your horse, so they never feel pain because of human ignorance, and finally horsemanship is about the end result of hard work, a quiet ride on a warm summers day with the sun peeking in and out of the trees, and a cooling breeze that floats your way; to feel the power of muscle under your seat, yet feel the softness of fine sleek hair through your fingers, to know that you have created a partnership that is forever.

Shelly Hamilton
Ontario, Canada
Proprietor of Spirit Horse Farm
Instructor of Horses 101
www.horse101fromthegroundup.com

For me the greatest experience is when you are in a show or just riding and you really feel you and you horses are in proper balance and harmony together. What a beautiful experience. I have felt this many times with my horses over the years. Horsemanship means you have mastered the techniques of success and what works with you and your horses. It takes a lifetime of practice. I am still learning. Now training a horse is a challenge. Mastering those techniques is really special. It is exciting to train horses. I am in the process of learning how everyday. You must have incredible patience. I do. I will go the extra mile and save our wild horses. We must leave a legacy.

Judith Hamilton-Schultze
Florida, USA
CEO/President, Equine Community Organization, Natural Organic World, LLC

Among all the sights of the docks, the noble truck-horses are not the least striking to a stranger. They are large and powerful brutes, with such sleek and glossy coats, that they look as if brushed and put on by a valet every morning. They march with a slow and stately step, lifting their ponderous hoofs like royal Siam elephants. Thou shalt not lay stripes upon these Roman citizens; for their docility is such, they are guided without rein or lash; they go or come, halt or march on, at a whisper. So grave, dignified, gentlemanly, and courteous did these fine truck-horses look - so full of calm intelligence and sagacity, that often I endeavored to get into conversation with them, as they stood in contemplative attitudes while their loads were preparing. But all I could get from them was the mere recognition of a friendly neigh; though I would stake much upon it that, could I have spoken in their language, I would have derived from them a good deal of valuable information touching the docks, where they passed the whole of their dignified lives.

Herman Melville, *Redburn. His First Voyage,* 1849

Harmony with the horse: that is to say: Having the humility to know that as a rider or horse owner you don't know it all, whilst working on broadening your equestrian knowledge from all available sources to increase your experience and maximize on the relationship you have with your horse or horse in the most positive and fun way possible.

Dany Hancock
Botswana
Professional Horsewoman
Horseback Riding Tour Guide
www.ridesonthewildside.com

Just as the name implies, the horse comes first. And no doubt because of my childhood experience with USPC, the word to me brings immediate images of horse care. To others it may be about equitation or riding skill, but in my mind, if you take great care of your horse through conditioning and nutrition, performance excellence follows. Don't laugh, but when I was Cosequin WEF Circuit Champion, one of my biggest expenses was carrots! Every time my horse Riviera City saw me coming, he knew he was going to get a carrot. Always had one in my pocket after he cooled off from a jump-off too. He tried very hard for me.

James Hastie
Past Cosequin Winter Equestrian Festival Circuit Champion
Executive Director, Thoroughbred Aftercare Alliance Foundation
www.ThoroughbredAftercare.org

Horsemanship to me is a way to describe a relationship between a human being and a horse, which I believe is identical to a relationship between two humans. What I've learned is that in a human relationship, whether it's a husband/wife, parent/child, or best friends, there are three ingredients that have to be present for the relationship to work - love, trust and respect. In order to have a healthy, happy relationship you must have all three.

If I love and respect my wife, but I don't trust her, the relationship won't work. The same is true for horses. If I love and respect my horse but I don't trust him because when I go for a ride I'm worried I might get bucked off, we're also not going to have a good relationship. If my horse respects me, loves me, but doesn't trust me because he thinks that every time he does something I don't like I am going to hit, whip or spur him, our relationship isn't going to work either.

Horsemanship is based upon love, trust and respect between a horse and a human. In the end, the same golden rule that you and I were taught is exactly what is needed in horsemanship. We want to treat our horses the same way we want to be treated.

Tim Hayes
Natural Horsemanship Instructor
Author of *Riding Home – The Power of Horses to Heal*
www.hayesisforhorses.com

What does horsemanship mean to you?

Two things: 1) a commitment to lifelong learning to be a better partner to your horse and 2) putting your horse and his welfare first, always.

Cathy Herbert
Virginia, USA
Equestrian
Past Senior Editor of *Practical Horseman* and *Horse & Rider*
Author of *Shine On! Shiny Bits of Wisdom*

Mutual respect. I see little purpose in abuse of horses – an unhappy horse will never perform its best. They are the most generous and gentle of beasts and given the chance they will do their best for us (most of the time!). Take a moment to think – here is this half-ton animal; it could knock me flat, trample me to death, its physicality is such that it would win every fight a human challenged it to, yet instead of doing this, the horse chooses to comply to our demands and wishes. It carries us on its back for our pleasure, entertainment, in work and into battle and submits to mastery. How can such a submission not be respected?

Hannah Hooton
Ely, UK
Equestrian
Author of the *Aspen Valley Series*
www.hannahhootonbooks.blogspot.co.uk

Rainbow, Joe Stentzel, and Hobby. 1963
Greenville, Ohio USA
Photo Courtesy Peggy Jo Clark

The complete understanding of your horse at that moment you are competing on it. You have to know when it is tired, due to being cold, over exercised, over fed, under fed, has sore teeth or a sore back. There are many people who can ride and say they are horse people but there are very few who are true champions of it. It takes patience, time and fundamentally some people are born with it and others not. You can only learn so much, the rest is either a part of you or not.

Clare Hudson
United Kingdom
Polo Player, Clare Hudson Designs
www.clarehudsondesigns.co.uk

Horsemanship is to love, commit, understand and always be patient 24/7. Horse sense comes naturally if you are fortunate. Horses have always been my first priority and I have a family that understands those priorities.

Peter J. Hurst
World Equestrian, Poet
Author of *Horse Daze: My Time with Horses*

As a cattleman and a writer, horsemanship, to me, goes way beyond the disciplines of riding – whether it's in the arena, the show ring, or out on the range. I can tell you without a doubt, horsemanship is a personal, and in many cases a spiritual, journey between a horse and a human where the destination, for those who reach it, is a special kind of love and understanding that only makes sense to those who have traveled that bumpy road.

Here's a quote from my first novel. This can be said of most good cowboys and cowgirls I've known...

By nature, he is a horseman. Afoot he appears somehow incomplete and, in his presence, the horse appears incomplete without him – as though the hand that created him created the horse with him in mind.

D.B. Jackson
California, USA
Author of *They Rode Good Horses*
www.dalebjackson.com

This is the hardest question of all because horsemanship to me means more than just one person's relationship with his/her horse. I am currently reading *The Revolution in Horsemanship and What It Means to Mankind* by Rick Lamb and I agree with Lamb on many topics, but especially about how progressive/natural horsemanship is not about winning more ribbons or saddles, it's about the kind of people we are becoming. I'm a firm believer that how you treat your horse says a lot about who you are. To sum it up, horsemanship to me is about partnership and mutual understanding. If we could all incorporate those two things into our daily lives and relationships, we'd all be better people. Everyone who rides horses knows that horses teach you a lot more about yourself than anyone else every could, I just hope that one day everyone can learn how to effectively communicate with their horse in a way that never inspires fear or aggression.

Cody Jeffery
North Carolina, USA
Equestrian
www.happeningsinchina.weebly.com

Workhorse Doc, Bill Winstead, and W.C. Roberson
Farm of W. C. Roberson, Georgia USA. Circa 1950s
Photo Courtesy James Ignizio

Hmm this is a very fun question for me to answer. And I think the most important thing about horsemanship is to listen to your horse. They are not....just horses....as one person recently said to me. I don't even know what that means...just a horse. If I put a brush on a horse and they don't like it, I get a brush they do like. I don't force them to deal because they are just some dumb animal that has to submit to me. That does not work in the long run anyway. Some horses have skin that is extremely sensitive and if I want them to be happy with their work well I would really like for them to be happy while I am grooming them. I even had a horse once that did not want to be groomed until he was warmed up on some days. He had so much energy that he needed to move a bit before he could settle down and let a brush go on his body. And I was happy to listen to him when he told me that!

I care, I really care about how they feel. Now that does not mean that I will allow them to walk all over me, but some sure do try. They are huge happy well fed fit animals and they need intelligent, fair, caring, constant attention and training. They can't talk to us in words, sure, but they feel, have moods, fears, attitudes just like we do. Finding the job that suits them, makes "them" happy is important. You might have a horse that just screams Eventing all over it, but all he really wants to do is stay safe and cozy in a little ring jumping three-feet and nothing you can do no matter how good of a trainer you are can change that. You might have a classic Quarter Horse bred for cows and trail who is so spooky and I mean really afraid of things, that you take your life in your hands just going for a hack.

You might have a Pony with the heart of a lion and if they were bigger could be famous! Making sure that they have good dental work, proper fitting bits and saddles, worming, feet and correct feed for their body and workloads. Enough work that they are not going out of their mind with boredom or jumping out of their skin with access energy is key. Knowing when they need a prep day, or a push day or an easy day and not just "using" them because they are ....just a horse....that is what Horsemanship means to me.

Désirée Johnson
Proprietor of Smooth Stride Riding Wear USA
www.smoothstride.com

To me, horsemanship means working to achieve harmony between horse and rider in whatever discipline we choose to follow. I watched Charlotte Dujardin and Valegro at the 2012 London Olympics and I was bowled over by the lightness and sympathy of her riding.

Gill Kapadia
United Kingdom
Equestrian Writer, Freelance Photo Journalist
www.gillkapadia.co.uk/wordpress

A person that has the ability to connect with most any horses they come in contact with. Horses talk to us in their own way and horsemanship is being able to communicate back where they understand.

Jeff Klepinger
Florida, USA
Equine Dentist
www.equinedentist01.com

It's all about understanding a horse; to be around horses, understand horses, and they understand you. To be respectful is everything. It's all about respect. Once in a while I get horses I can't get along with. It's because they don't have respect; they don't trust people.

Bill Knowlton
Ohio, USA
Farrier

Horsemanship is... always thinking of the horse's best interest before your own.

Jennifer Malott Kotylo
Illinois, USA
Movement & Body Awareness Specialist for Equestrians
www.jenniferkotylo.com

First of all, real horsemanship isn't possible without connection in any discipline. I have learnt this with my own horse. I have had two accidents, and haven't been able to ride. I was wondering what I could do with my horse, I wanted to keep a relation with him, but I couldn't even take him for a walk or grazing. I had my knee broken, then a surgery, and a year after I had five ribs broken and lung perforated. I couldn't take the risk to get pulled by the rope if the horse moved his head too quick. So, I tried to work through "compartmental approach" at liberty, without being close to him at all. Connection is essential then!! And after that, I learnt that the connection you create, helps a lot in any equestrian discipline you practice.

Since I went to Mongolia, horsemanship has got a new meaning to me. Now, my way is mostly to stand with horses and learn from them. Not asking anything. Just studying their behavior, and trying to catch what they have to "tell" us, what they are telling from their link to universe. I also met Jean Francois Pignon and his horses recently. I have learnt a lot from him. The possibility of getting things from horses just with "talking-horse". We often try to make the horse learn things from us, but we do it with the language we think horses can understand. Maybe this is not wrong, but what I am sure of now, is that it is not the more direct and efficient way. This way is to learn how to talk-horse. Jean Francois Pignon shows evidence of this. It is so rich and full of emotions! It feeds my creativity.

Frédérique Lavergne
France
Fine Artist and Equestrian
www.frederiquelavergne.com

Horsemanship is the knowledge to have a horse perform a discipline to the best of its ability with the use of kindness.

Fred Kunkle
Arizona, USA
Equestrian
www.goldenwingshorseshoes.com

SWR Ghulam Jan Khan, British Indian Army Calvary
France, World War I. Circa 1914
Photo Courtesy Omer Tarin

Horsemanship is the relationship established between a human and a horse with mutual respect and trust. It's a partnership with the human being a kind and loving leader.

Penelope Langley
Tennessee, USA
Author and Equestrian
www.pennycandyproductions.com

Horsemanship, to many, is how well someone rides or handles a horse. To me, horsemanship is the ability one has to create, maintain and demonstrate a true partnership with a horse through understanding, kindness and mutual respect, rather than through force. Most anyone can prove to an animal that the world is a more pleasant place if they just give in and do as demanded, but it takes much more to forge the enduring bond that comes from true horsemanship. A lifelong bond that allows the two to act as one cohesive unit.

Lynne Levy
Wisconsin, USA
Equestrian, Horse Trainer Clinician, Horse Show Judge (Retired)

Horsemanship is knowing your horse inside out.

Gaby Lucas
Chelmsford, United Kingdom
International Equestrian
World Class Dressage Development Programme
www.gab-iiy.wix.com/gabylucas

For me, horsemanship, or being a good horse-man/woman, is pretty simple: take good care of your horse's physical needs, keep your mind open to learning new ways to better train and/or communicate with your equine partner, and don't impose human emotions and thoughts onto your horse. I've heard people say things like "my horse hates me," or "that horse is such a bitch," or "my horse is testing my patience today." Horses are smart, some are clever, but they aren't human, thank God. It would make for better equine/human relation-ships if the human tried to think more like the horse when in the saddle instead of assuming the horse is thinking/feeling human thoughts and emotions.

TK Lukas
Texas, USA
Equestrian
Author of *Orphan Moon*
www.tklukas.com

What does horsemanship mean to you?

I was taught to ride by an old Aussie woman named Kanga who taught real horsemanship. I never knew anything else until I got older and saw the different ways people did things. I would like to teach my grandkids like Kanga taught me! Respect for the horse was always number one!

Roni McFadden
California, USA
Equestrian
Author of *The Longest Trail* and *Josephine*
www.thebiscuitpress.com

I guess it means being firm and gentle, spending the time trying to shape up the outside while searching for that connection on the inside.

Barbara Meikle
New Mexico, USA
Fine Artist
www.meiklefineart.com

To me, it has a couple of meanings. One more direct, as in, the Western Horsemanship classes we used to compete in, where the judging is based on the rider's performance, often with a pattern to perform, and rail work. The other, more general, meaning a person's overall equine skill set. If someone displays good horsemanship, they handle horses well, and themselves well around horses.

Karen Melroy
Ohio, USA
Equine Blogger
www.equineinmind.wordpress.com

Horsemanship to me is about learning to be the best advocate for the equine species that I can. It means being able to read a horse's body language, look after their health and know when something is wrong and work to correct it. It also means constantly learning about them.

Christine Meunier
Wangaratta, Victoria, Australia
Equestrian, Author, Endurance Rider, Horse Trainer
Author of *Horse Country*
www.horsecountrybook.com

The definition of horsemanship is basically the skill, art or practice of riding horses. What it means to me is love. Pure love. Love of a beast that is so big he can squash you like a grape...but won't...because he loves you, too.

Karen Miscovich
Florida, USA
Optimal Horse Environment Horse Boarding at Picalata Farms

To me, horsemanship means a sense of pride and accomplishment. It is being among kindred spirits. It is chance to be near the most beautiful gentle and loving creatures you could ever meet. For me, riding a horse is pure freedom and nothing short of complete peace.

Amber Moore
Author of *Bartender Tales*
www.authorambermoore.com

Horsemanship means partnership to me, really. To have good horsemanship one has to establish a real partnership with a horse so that the horse understands you, you understand your horse, and you do what you do together, with both of you happy about it! Physically willing to do what you are doing; which means without fear or intimidation. I am a big believer of natural horsemanship; the days of spurs, jerking, and intimidation, in my opinion, are over. We are past that. To me, horsemanship means partnership.

Elaine Nash
New York City, USA
Proprietor and Founder of Fleet of Angels
Providing safe passage for at-risk equines.
www.fleetofangels.org

Horsemanship, to me, means communication, with love, which flows both ways between a person and the horses she meets. Horsemanship is an endless process of learning and practicing, which leads to growth and development of the skills that allow horses to understand the horseman, as the horseman gradually learns to better understand the horse. We who would be horsemen know that we are fortunate to have the love and companionship of these beautiful athletes. There is no thrill greater than those found on the back of a willing and well-trained horse, who executes your wishes almost before you have time to translate them into requests. The true horseman doesn't need to think about how to ask the horse to do something; he or she just rides the horse and thinks about doing the thing, whether it is sidepass, piaffe, or turning back a cow ... and the trained horse feels the intention in the hands, the legs, the seat of the rider, and executes the movement with willingness, impulsion, and confidence. True horsemanship is seen when the horse and the rider perform as one, and it is beautiful to watch.

Angela Norton
Texas, USA
Proprietor, Diamond Magic Arabians
www.diamondmagicarabians.com

Horsemanship is a big part to every event. There has to be a foundation between you and your horse. No foundation, no connection. Horsemanship comes down to your hands to your feet, every part of you has to be working together in the right way to get what you want your horse to do. I am still working on my horsemanship because I do not know everything and I am always learning how to improve my skills. It is a never-ending journey with horsemanship.

Shelby Osceloa
Alabama, USA
Equestrian and National Rodeo Competitor

Horsemanship in the dictionary is shown as the "art, ability and skill in handling and riding horses." To me, horsemanship is this and so much more. It is being a team with the horse, working as one, like true dance partners in step with each other. Horsemanship and horseman or horse persons show a true love of horses for the unique animals they are.

Lynette Partridge-Schneider
Illinois, USA
Founder/Proprietor, Quail Ridge Equine, Equine Appraiser
www.quailridgeequine.com

To me, my horse is my trainer and a partner. If you can understand your horse and learn from him, both will be in perfect harmony; be gentle, patient and caring. You also need to spend time with your horse, not just only when you are riding, but when he is inside the stall, when he is grazing, and when he is in the paddock. A well-trained horse is a blessing very few can have.

Saif Patel
Vancouver, British Colombia
Equestrian, Photographer
www.saifpatelphotography.com

Tawny O'Hara, 6-years-old, and Silver
Beaver County, Oklahoma.
Photo Courtesy Tawny O'Hara, New Mexico, USA

Horsemanship is... getting a real partnership between horse and rider, being able to totally trust as well as control your mount.

David Puckey
Oxford, United Kingdom
Captain, RLC Tentepegging Team (Army)
Training Officer, British Tentpegging
European Coordinator, World Tentpegging Federation
www.britishtentpegging.com

Horsemanship is more to me than technical ability or skill. True horsemanship separates people who just ride horses (albeit very well), from people who truly know and respect their equine partners. Horsemanship involves teamwork, connection, mindset, generosity, a desire to constantly learn, and the willingness to set an example for other riders and horse owners. Horsemanship, to me, is a reflection of the same noble qualities that horses themselves possess.

DK Raymer
Missouri, USA
Author of *Lily's Song*
www.DKRaymer.com

Horsemanship is learning everything you can about the horse, and then doing everything you can to give the horse the best and most productive life possible. There is no limit to horsemanship. It's about listening, learning, and becoming the most humble and also the most assertive person you can possibly be. You have to know when you are the alpha and when you are the partner. It's all about the good of the horse.

Natalie Keller Reinert
Equestrian and Equine Writer
Author of Other People's Horses
www.nataliekreinert.com

Horsemanship means to me the ability to earn their trust, build a relationship, become a team and to truly understand what he thinks. Respect them and never lose patience. Sam and I love what we do! We love horses so much and feel so lucky to be able to do what we do. We work very, very hard, but it is all worth it. I feel like horses make us better people, everyday spent with our horses is a great day.

One of my most favorite quotes by Ronald Duncan... *The horse. Here is nobility without conceit, friendship without envy, beauty without vanity. A willing servant, yet never a slave.*

Kelly and Sam Rettinger
Ohio, USA
Whispery Pines Carriage Rides & Logging
www.whisperypinescarriagerideslogging.com

Wow! That question snuck up on me ... what an interesting, important question. Well, the first word that popped into my head was "respect" and I mean that on many levels. We need to respect the power of horses, and we also need to respect how they like to be treated – which, often, is in opposition to their power. They respond so well to subtlety and kindness.

I think, once you have respect, the rest falls into place. It makes you want to learn more about your horse – his health, the environment that works best for him, his training – and as you learn more about all aspects, your horsemanship is developing.

Sometimes riding is involved, and sometimes not, but I'm going to borrow a corporate term (and one I don't usually like) and say good horsemanship is a striving for "best practices" with regards to your particular horse and his needs.

Tudor Robins
Ontario, Canada
Equestrian, Author of *Appaloosa Summer*
www.tudorrobbins.ca

I once met a horse at a boarding stable who was just freed into an outdoor enclosure before its training session. I was enlightened by its spiritedness - it being an anxious hot-blood from the Arabian Peninsula... Its dark dappled presence fronted with me and he flexed its neck and head and his eyes as strangely as they would go. I was his challenger - me, the spectator at the fence - to a dusty race across the pen with his flared nose held airborne and either eye glaring at mine at every turn, and both ears in constant swivel. Ebony was the mane that fluttered wild in every stride and fractious was the tail followed; a gallop, a prance, an improvised trot, a strut, a jagged halt - that was meant to assess my willingness to spar or cowardess. I remained calm, but breathed through my nose with reverence of the equine deity in my presence. He rounded his fourth turn and that was all he needed, for he ceased his motion and stopped tall in the middle of the pen, and his dust cleared. An astounding being in horse flesh - eyes as deep in tone as his neck, nose splotched pink at the lip, ears alive and ready on his head. I saw him vividly for the first time. And he allowed me to stay. We inhaled and exhaled with symbiosis, and the planet did silence around us. I took the moment to finally blink, and the horse chewed the grass in his mouth.

Anthony Valentino Robinson
Ohio, USA
Fine Artist
www.anthonyathiseasel.com

My horsemanship means the world, simply because I am striving hard to be a part of a good beneficial solution for horses and people, rather than become another problem for both due to misleading information out there.

Horsemanship is about being responsible for the welfare of the horse. That's at the forefront. It's not about getting your horse to do A, B, or C. True horsemanship is about the betterment of the horse. Two species coming together is a remarkable thing. I think we need to remember that we are the ones calling all the shots though. We need to ensure the horse is content and comfortable. Relaxation is a big thing for me. If a horse isn't relaxed, then he's stressed. There must be a physical or mental issue that needs to be addressed. Whatever the problem, dealing with it is our responsibility. Becoming knowledgeable so we can prevent problems is important too. There's a lot of blaming the horse for things. When people say this horse is stupid, or stubborn, or mean, or whatever, I think it's always unfair to the horse. We don't always know what's going on with the horse. I have horses that I work with that when they're cranky the client blames the horse. I worked with a client just last week who said, "My horse is in a bad mood today, I don't know what her deal is, can you help me?" She was frustrated about the horse. I asked if it was a new behavior or is she like this all the time. "No, she's not like this all the time, but, boy, she's having a bad day." Especially if a behavior is out of the ordinary, it's likely something is bothering her or she needs help. So, the client brought the horse over and I could see her front feet were sore. She had laminitis; she was hurting. Horsemanship is thinking about it from the horse's point of view and not jumping to conclusions.

Dale Rudin
Tennessee, USA
Equestrian, Horse Trainer and Clinician
Certified Horsemanship Association Riding Instructor
Founder of Unnatural Horsemanship®
www.Un-NaturalHorsemanship.com

Horsemanship means having a relationship with horses that allows mutual respect.

Katie Ryan
California, USA
Equine Assisted Therapist
Author of *Horse Wisdom Alchemy*
www.horsewisdomalchemy.com

Horsemanship to me is the art of listening to what the horses have to tell us (through their actions, the look in their eyes). Whether it be in the saddle or on the ground. Animals always have something to say, if we look and listen close we will hear it and it will make for a better relationship.

Tamara Rymer
Texas, USA
Equestrian, Fine Artist
www.tamararymer.com

I would say that horsemanship to me means loving the hobby and loving the horses, you don't have to be a cowboy or a pro rider, you just need to enjoy the horse and treat them well and the horse will enjoy you. People need to know that horses need to trust the people that ride them as much as the people need to trust the horse they ride.

Tom Sandmeyer
Minnesota, USA
Horse Lover

Horsemanship means love, compassion, patience and understanding along with your knowledge and experience. You need all of these together to have horsemanship in my humble opinion. Horses are so willing to do what you ask, when you ask and don't demand. We often tell them to do something completely against their nature- that is a huge mistake. I love them to be who they are - magnificent beings!

Vicki Sims
California, USA
President/Founder Sadie's Haven Horse Rescue & Sanctuary
www.sadieshaven.org

To me, horsemanship, is having the ability to establish and then develop a productive relationship with a horse, which subsequently leads to earning the horse's trust and confidence in you.

Bill Slader
Ohio, USA
Equine Photographer
www.billsladerphotography.com

Horsemanship is a partnership between human and equine where a person learns to speak to a horse using their language which also teaches communication. It's like learning a whole new language and having patience with an open mind and heart. This is what horsemanship means to me.

Caitlin Lorraine Smith
Oregon, USA
Equestrian & Equine Rescue Advocate

Horsemanship is about being willing to listen to your horse and adapt what YOU DO to what the horse needs. People apply HUMAN values to horses and that is not valid. Horses try so hard to do what we ask, try asking in a way the horse understands. How you THINK controls what you do and who you are. Be willing to change how you think to help your horse. Build a partnership, with you as the lead partner. And lastly, get past the industry obsession with tack and other equipment. Much of that gets in the way of having a better relationship with your horse. Consider the Native Americans – they would ride all over the roughest terrain in the US, and even fought WARS on horseback. And they did it with no horseshoes, no bits, no saddles, no spurs, etc. etc. And people today cannot get their horse to walk through a puddle!!!!! The horse industry has not progressed much, to the benefit of the horse. Their commercial success is incredible, selling stuff you really don't need. And it is really not good for the horses. If you do something that is not good for your horse, but you don't know that, it does NOT make it any easier on the horse! Horsemanship is about doing what is best for the horse. Period. And what is best for the horse is always best for you too!

Dan Sumerel
Virginia, USA
Founder of *Sumerel Training* and *Sumerel Therapy*
Author of *Finding the Magic*
www.sumereltraining.com

My horsemanship means the world, simply because I am striving hard to be a part of a good beneficial solution for horses and people, rather than become another problem for both due to misleading information out there.

Carlos Tabernaberri
Victoria, Australia
Horse Trainer and Clinician
Proprietor of Whispering Acres
www.whisperingacres.com

For me, horsemanship is a mindful way of life. Orzel's rider, my friend and mentor Shelley Groom Trevor, maintains that "the rider you are is the person you are." You can see this every day in how we relate with horses; they are definitely our mirrors, if we allow ourselves to look. In Tibetan Buddhism there is a concept called *lungta,* which translates as "windhorse" — representing the strength, energy, endurance and dignity of the horse. We humans can cultivate these qualities; as Buddhists put it, we can "raise windhorse." The first time I took part in a Tibetan windhorse-raising practice, it was immediately familiar to me - it's the profound, uplifted quality you feel when you're near horses. Every day, whether I am cleaning stalls, or stacking hay, or doing a flying change, I can't help but reflect on how fortunate we are to live closely with these amazing creatures, these windhorses.

Horsemanship is also about taking good care of our horses throughout the course of their lives. In that vein, among the many wonderful horse nonprofits out there, I'd like to mention the great work by Brooke USA, which focuses on helping working equines in impoverished communities throughout the world, where "horsepower" is still the primary means of transportation. Horses have given me so much over the years; it's a privilege to be able to help them where I can.

Tobi Lopez Taylor, M.A.
Writer, Editor, Anthropologist
Author of *Orzel*
www.TobiTaylor.com

Horsemanship means to me, the knowledge about the horse, so not only in the show arena, but more in the everyday time you spent with the horses understanding that these beautiful creatures are willing to put up with us humans, which are at the same time often their biggest problem. The moment some one realizes that they are the biggest problem a horse can have, and willing to learn not to be that, and establish the best possible relationship based on trust, tranquility and respect and responsibility, that is what horsemanship means to me.

Zeliha Thomas
Netherlands
Co-Proprietor Crown Quarter Horses
FEI and NRHA Western Trainer
Reining, Pleasure, Trail, and Horsemanship Expert
www.crownquarterhorses.jouwweb.nl

I love being around horse people. I can be a real talker and I think the first thing that hit me during my first lunch at the ranch's lodge was how quiet the "barn table" could be. We would joke and tease like the other tables but there were often long lulls in the conversation that for the first time in my life didn't feel like awkward silence. I think that speaks to the depth of being a horseman, that so much of your time with horses is spent in non-verbal communication that you are that much more of a thinker, and you become so competent at working out situations internally that words aren't always necessary. I love that.

Jayne Thurber-Smith
Virginia, USA
Equestrian & Freelance Writer

For me horsemanship is first understanding that a horse is and always will be a horse!! Never should a horse to be compared to a human, they are a different species and do not have the same thought process. Then being able to develop a positive relationship between horse and human. Good horsemen/women have an understanding and a special talent in working with horses without the necessity for dominance, aggression or severe punishment. Being able to teach a horse well, have healthy human/horse boundaries and have a horse willingly attempt to do all that is asked for. Communicating with horses is part of having good horsemanship skills, communicating oneself clearly with the horse so that it understands what is being asked of it, and recognizing what the horse wants to communicate. Being able to respond accordingly and without instilling fear. We need to respect horses and at the same time receive respect from horses. Horse have an amazing ability and willingness to learn, which means they can also be taught not to perform undesirable behavior. That being said, often undesirable behaviors are communication tools that are misunderstood. As with almost everything, some people have a natural talent and gift for bringing out the best in horses, usually they are good horsemen/women!

Adrienne Tomkinson
World Equestrian
Founder and Proprietor of ImPuls Methode™
www.impuls-methode.at

I grew up with horses and I was a keen showjumper up until my late teens. My mother still has horses and I always go riding with her when I go home to visit. She lives in Yorkshire and keeps her horses on a yard which is part of the Harewood estate where I grew up. It is such a beautiful part of the world and I dream about having my own horse again. There is plans very near in the future to buy a racehorse, something which I have in the pipeline at the moment.

Caroline Towning
London, England
Contemporary Equestrian Artist
www.carolinetowning.com

Horsemanship means... to be able to communicate with another species.

Stavros Vergis
Athens, Greece
Equestrian and Horse Trainer

Most of us will never win a silver cup or perform airs above the ground. Even if we do, for me, horsemanship starts with responsible care and stewardship. It is a willingness to continue to learn and improve riding skills in order to keep both horse and rider safe. It is patience and grace under stress. It is turning the me into we on entering the barn.

Candace Wade
Tennessee, USA
Equestrian, Co-Author of *Horse Sluts*
www.candacewade.com

"Me and my mates riding through Nimbin
on a rather wet day 25 odd years ago."
Photo Courtesy Stavros Steve Vergis
Equestrian and Trainer, Greece

Stavros Vergis (left), Equestrian and Horse Trainer
Endurance ride with Digger.
Photo Courtesy Stavros Vergis

I would say that being a cowboy one must always be respectful of others. A good horseman/woman takes care of his animal first and last. That horse has a special relationship with nature and you. Respect it and it will respect you. Be good to fellow riders, treat them like you want to be treated. Understand that others have opinions that may not reflect yours, as long as no one is in danger a simple forced smile and a nod is all you really need to do. Then ride on.

Gary Winstead
California, USA
Author, Writer, Actor, Movie Producer and Director
Author of *Murder in Auburn*
www.crimsoncloakpublishing.com/gary-winstead.html

Horsemanship to me means much more than what we do with horses. Now that I am seventy years old, I finally learned that horsemanship is something that teaches us much in our lives. When I look back over the many years of buying, selling, competing, showing, and breeding, I realize that the people we all meet in the horse business matter greatly. We make lifelong friends, and we learn from those friends as much as we do from horsemanship. About thirty-five years ago I owned the world champion calf roping horse and didn't make any money to speak of when all of the bills were paid. That experience got me into racing horses. And, that experience eventually got me into breeding, so somehow or another, it seems to all go hand-in-hand, but one thing is for sure - the people we meet in the horse business, no matter which part of the business they are in, are the ones we remember as much as the horses. My sister is sixty-six years old and she is still in the barrel racing business, buying and selling and training barrel horses. Horsemanship in many ways is much like a college education. It teaches us much that cannot be written in books, but that is written in life.

Mike Yarbro
Mississippi, USA
Equestrian
Past Barrel Racer, Roper, Horse Breeder, Showman
Author of *Champion's Heart*
www.mikeyarbro.com

Horsemanship to me feels sacred, it's this never-ending way of life where I strive day in and day out to be better for the horse and with the horse. For whatever reason, I have been drawn to the horse my whole life and there's this higher level of understanding that I want to reach. Within horsemanship it is well known that you will never know it all, you're constantly learning and understanding the horse in new ways, I believe that's what is so addicting about it that I can keep learning, I can reach new levels of communication with the horse. Horsemanship is enlightening, challenging and incredibly rewarding. When one even learns the basics of horsemanship, a whole new world opens and you notice your horse is so much different, better, now that you are being let on to this language that was once dismissed in place of barbaric training methods. To have a mutual, working relationship with an animal as large as the horse - who we shouldn't really in the first place - is in every sense of the word magical. To practice horsemanship to me is a religious experience and I encourage everyone to learn and practice horsemanship in everything they do with their horse.

Devin Young
Ohio, USA
Proprietor of Painted Lady Horsemanship
www.paintedladyranch.wix.com/paintedladyhorseman

Horsemanship
Quotes from Riders Around the World

Are you a horseman or horsewoman who would like to share the joys of horsemanship? We would love to hear from you! *What does horsemanship mean to you?* Send your answer to mondaycreekpublishing@gmail.com and you will be included in *Horsemanship: Quotes from Riders Around the World, Volume II*!

Monday Creek Publishing is honored to donate a portion of the proceeds from this book to local horse rescues, as well as support local youth equestrians.

www.mondaycreekpublishing.com

Horsemanship
Quotes from Riders Around the World

What does horsemanship mean to you?

Gina McKnight
Author, Freelancer, Equestrian, and Poet

Living in the foothills of the Appalachian Mountains promotes inspiration and passion for creative writing; children's literature, poetry, freelance, and more. Gina is a Leadership Scholar/Bachelor of Arts, Franklin University, Ohio USA.Her poetry has appeared in international anthologies and literary journals. Her first volume of poetry *To the Heart* was released in 2015. In her second volume, *Poetry from the Field*, she affirms her love of life, nature, and intangible gifts.

Children's literature includes *The Blackberry Patch* (2009), *Trail Ride to Snake Hollow* (2018 Monday Creek Publishing), *Nawaab: Marwari Stallion of India Series* (2017 Banyan Publishing India). Gina is also the author of *Dr. Abbott "Pete" Smith, DVM, the Official Biography* (2017 Monday Creek Publishing).

And award-winning blogger, Gins is also a freelance writer, currently a regular contributor to *Florida Equine Athlete*, and *Arabian Finish Line*. She loves her horses; Paint mare, Zubedia, and Quarter Horse gelding, Charming N Arrogant, aka Mac.

Zorka Veličković
Fine Artist

Illustrator's Note

For my son who always trusted in me and for all the beautiful horses of India who touched my heart, for all magic moments which remains forever. I was drawing horses since my early childhood. My father was an artist, very successful one, I learned from him a lot, not only about techniques in painting, but more about hard work, dedication and sacrifice for art. After seeing my first Marwari - nukra named Swraj - from Punjab, I started a new chapter in life/ I finally found eternal inspiration in those horses from far away. I rarely paint only horses, usually I use a lot of ornaments and vivid colors to underscore significance and emotions of my models on four legs. Many people ask from where I use all my motifs and ornaments - they look like from ancient times in India. I adore Mughal art from the time they ruled India, and I find inspiration in it but never to copy them. All my work is definitely originated in my soul and heart... origin of my soul seems to be in that old, ancient times when beauty of nature was celebrated by the hands of old masters painting. Like then, I also use mostly pigment colors with gum arabica dissolved in sea shells. Illustrating this book was great chance for me to escape back in childhood days and enjoy in painting imaginary world from the past using that ancient technique.

About the Illustrator

Zorka Veličković, is a self-taught artist from Serbia. She lives in the small town Kragujevac, in part of the country called Woodland. She is a mother of a 22 year old son and works as an Elementary school teacher. From 2011 she has dedicated her art exclusively to painting and promoting horses of Indian breeds - Marwaris and Kathiawaris, and horses of Pakistan. Her paintings are mostly in private collections worldwide; she holds permanent exhibition in a restaurant gallery at the local race court in her town. Her art was part of the endurance event at Sikar 2015. Her paintings were the official promotional poster at same event. Zorka has visited India three times, where she was guest and visitor of many respectful horse farms at Punjab and Rajasthan. In the last five years of her art work, she painted more than a thousand famous and less famous, but beautiful Indian horses.

www.ingramcontent.com/pod-product-compliance
Lightning Source LLC
Chambersburg PA
CBHW050353280326
41933CB00010BA/1452